Finding
You
in
Every Script

An Actor's Guide on How to Create Characters
& Get Booked Being Authentically You

Shaunté Massard

Publishing Services: Pen Legacy, LLC (www.penlegacy.com)
Interior Images: Dhar Mann Studios
Cover Creation: Christian Cuan
Editing and Formatting: Carla M. Dean, U Can Mark My Word

Library of Congress Cataloging – in- Publication Data has been applied for.

ISBN: 979-8-986377-0-3

PRINTED IN THE UNITED STATES OF AMERICA.

First Edition

Testimonials

"Shaunté Massard is an extraordinary actress who is so inspiring to work with."

— Dhar Mann, Entrepreneur
Content creator with over 35 billion views

"Shaunté is aligned with her calling as an actress. Align with her and you will find your path as well."

— Marie-Francoise Theodore, Actress
Only Murders in the Building,
The Young and the Restless, and Love Jones

"Shaunté is not only an amazing actress, she's also a coach and mentor who wants to see you win!"

— Saundra Charleston, Actress
Co-author of *A Reason to Be: Seeking Life Purpose*

"I'm so inspired by Shaunté's connection to life, relationships, and the world of acting. She is incredible at her craft and amazing at what she does."

— Jennifer Inniss Eastmond, Director
Author, Founder & CEO of Boss Life Mastery

Dedication

This book is dedicated
To every artist with a burden to be seen,
to be heard, and to create.
You are more than enough.
Take up your space.
You are the answer.
Be authentically you.

Acknowledgements

To my Lord and Savior, Jesus Christ, the author and finisher of my faith. Because of You, I am redeemed. I am no longer who I used to be. I am a Child of God. I am a new creation. *2 Cor. 5:17*

To my husband, my patna', my King, Doc, for leaving everything you were familiar with and everyone you knew to move to California and become one with me on this crazy adventure. Thanks so much for holding on tight and providing the love and support I desperately needed but didn't know I did. I can't thank you enough. Mostess.

To Milaan, for trusting me to be your mom and giving me a reason to grow up and find my purpose. Thank you.

To Nassir, for truly believing that your mom can be and do anything. Thank you.

To Josiah, for proclaiming being "birthed and raised by the mother of the century," which means more to me than anything else in this world. Thank you.

To Khai Zion, for inspiring your G-ma to create a prosperous future for generations to come.

To Mom and Freddie, Dad and Johnyell, Grandma and Granddad Manning, Grandma and Granddad Telesford, my awesome aunts, uncles, brothers, sisters, cousins, extended DC fam and LA fam, thank you all for loving me.

To Dhar Mann, the Dhar fam, besties, followers, and fans on Instagram, TikTok, Facebook, and YouTube, I can't thank you enough for all the love, kind words, artwork, postings, encouragement, praise, and appreciation for the work that I love to do.

Table of Contents

Finding *You* in Every Script

An Actor's Guide on How to Create Characters & Get Booked Being Authentically You

Introduction

Wait a minute! I'm getting paid to kiss *thee* Lance Gross from Tyler Perry's long-running series *House of Payne*! Life doesn't get much better than this. But wait! Next stop… *And the Academy Award goes to (insert dramatic pause) Shaunté Massard!* How did this come about, you ask? Allow me to share with you a little backdrop.

When I was growing up, some would say my family was crazy, and by "some," I'm referring to myself. In my mind, I was the only sane one. I just didn't understand why some of my family members would repeatedly do the negative things they did, only to get the same negative results. I couldn't figure them out; it made no sense to me at all.

When I went to college the first time (that's another story for another book), I planned to study psychology. My thought process was that I could use the knowledge gained to help my family fix whatever made them so despondent, angry, and, well, just downright mean. However, when I started college, I discovered my true love—acting!

It's funny because, as a young girl, I was terrified of performing in front of people, but at the same time, I loved being creative through acting and singing. Then, when I went away to college, I no longer had the responsibility of being my family's savior and could allow myself to be me. I quickly went from wanting to study psychology to studying acting. However, I soon realized psychology and acting were very similar, especially in two ways.

The first is that "acting is healing to the soul and mind." It offers an escape from life as we have experienced it. It makes you laugh; it makes you cry. It's cathartic. The second is, in acting, there is research that you must do to find out why a character might do the things they do or say to accomplish their objective.

Transitioning from psychology into acting was easy, but it wasn't until years later that my pastor friend introduced me to Enneagrams for the purpose of understanding myself and others. Enneagrams are an ancient numeric personality type system. This ancient tool is used for personal understanding, development, and transformation. It helps people understand who they are and how they tick. Knowing the different personality types of the people who you work with and love can improve those relationships.

It was then that I realized I could use this system in tandem with my acting training to help me quickly and efficiently break down my characters to give a compelling performance. This personality system opened a whole new world for me. I felt like I had found "the secret" to acting. It was about discovering who "I" am, with "I" being the character I portrayed in every story. After moving to Los Angeles, California, and working with Diana Castle at The Imagined Life Studio, she confirmed I was on the right track with discovering the "I am."

As an actor, I have tried many techniques to create a character when I am storytelling—whether in a play, a film, or on TV. Many swear by The Stanislavski Method, but it was emotionally exhausting for me. With his technique, you use "real-life" trauma to infuse "real" feelings into make-believe circumstances. But what if I don't want to think about my dog dying 20 years ago to cry in a scene about breaking up with my boyfriend or even in film enduring the hardship of slavery as a slave in 1809? (Yes, I was actually asked to do that by a director.)

Then there's the Meisner technique, which is much like improv, playing off what the other person is doing and saying in a scene. But what if he's not giving you anything——no emotion, no connection, or just bad acting? Then you're out there just paddling that boat all alone. (Been there, done that.)

The Enneagram personality system is an easy and much less emotionally painful way of creating a character because you're basing it on real emotional reactions without digging up your personal trauma. Reliving real-life trauma is why many actors go crazy; it can make a person manic depressive. Performing a scene is not worth the real-life pain, suffering, and misery of reliving past trauma. Although if you have received help through counseling with a professional and feel a sense of closure, you may be able to use the act of compartmentalizing those feelings for your work as an actor, and it will not affect your life in an unhealthy way. The wonderful thing about using this system is that when you find your personality type and use your toolbox of emotions in the story or the written imaginary circumstances also known as your script, this ultimately intensifies your acting career. This is the healing process that I went through, and it lead me to become a healthy artist creating fulfilling roles on platforms like Netflix, BET, and YouTube's Dhar Mann Studios.

Take, for instance, the character I played in Tyler Perry's *House of Payne*. Victoria was an older woman who was a real estate agent, recently divorced, attractive, and professional. Lance Gross's character, Calvin, was very attracted to "me" (Victoria) and made it clear to "me" that he was interested. Knowing what type of person "I am" and what type of person "Calvin" is brought the scene to life! It did not matter whether Lance Gross, the actor, and Shaunté Massard, the actor, were attracted to each other or not. "Calvin" and "Victoria" were on fire and had a burning desire for each other when "we" were together. I knew Victoria had a driven, get-the-job-done, no-time-for-feelings personality (Type 8 – The Challenger), while Calvin cooled "me" down with his chill, free-spirited, optimistic personality (Type 7 – The Optimist). This made for a finished product that thousands of viewers raved about in reviews and online. If you want these kinds of results, then stay tuned.

The Personality Breakdown

The breakdown of the following Enneagram personality types can help you find yourself in the works you create and in your real-life relationships.

Type 1: The Perfectionist
- "People have told me that I can be overly critical."
- "Details are very important to me."

Type 2: The Helper
- "I don't know how to say no."
- "I'm drawn to influential people."

Type 3: The Achiever
- "It's important for me to come across as a winner."
- "I am competitive to a fault."

Type 4: The Individualist
- "I never felt like I belonged."
- "I tend to hang back in social settings and let people come to me."

Type 5: The Observer

- "I take care of myself and feel others can do the same."
- "I don't like when people want too much information."

Type 6: The Skeptic

- "I'm always imagining and planning for the worse."
- "I act quickly in a crisis, but when things settle down, I tend to fall apart."

Type 7: The Optimist

- "I'm an optimist to a fault."
- "I suffer from FOMO—fear of missing out."

Type 8: The Challenger

- "Lead me, follow me, or get out of my way."
- "I have been told I am too blunt and aggressive."

Type 9: The Peacemaker

- "I'll do almost anything to avoid conflict."
- "I'm happy to go along with what others want to do."

If you see yourself in more than one category of these personality types, that's common. We all possess a few of these qualities, but the best way to better understand who you are is by honing in on your core personality type. In times of distress or even during complete relaxation, your primary personality type may blend with another personality type in order for you to adapt properly to any given environment. Culture, religion, and significant life experiences may also play a big part in how one shows up in the world.

Dr. Martin Luther King, Jr. is the perfect example of a blend of personality types 8 and 9—challenger and peacemaker.

Learning about personality types from online resources, podcasts, and books from experts like Suzanne Stabile, Ian Morgan Corn, and Noble Works got me excited when applying it to creating characters for my scripts. Also, by studying these personality types, I have been able to understand and accept myself and my family much better. I have found in my spiritual journey that we are "fearfully and wonderfully made." God made us all unique; however, there are some foundational similarities we share as humans. I get super empathetic when I'm discovering other personalities. Despite a person's idiosyncrasies, they are human beings with wants and needs, just like you and me. No matter our color, shape, size, economic status, or religious belief, we are all experiencing life as humans. We are different in beautiful ways, yet we are the same. I believe that once we realize this, our work will be relatable and make us better people to each other. I think the best actors already know it. When I used what I had learned about the personality types in my work, I got results, and I believe you can, too!

Honestly, using this personality type system isn't a proven science, but what I know for sure—it is fun. That's what I want you to do while experiencing this guide— Have fun! Disclaimer: I am not a psychologist, nor am I a therapist. My role here is not to diagnose you or your family members. I only want you to see how you can be enlightened and, as a result, open yourself up to seeing and understanding people and yourself in a different way or confirm what you already knew. So, give it a try. See which types fit you, your loved ones, your characters, or the new people you meet and want to meet. As for me, I will continue to utilize this knowledge of varying personality types to help me figure out the relationships that can amplify my life and my career. And to all the actors and aspiring actors who are taking the time to read my book, thank you. I am looking forward to sharing an amazing acting experience with you on set or on stage one day soon.

"The great gift of human beings is that we have the power of empathy."

~ Meryl Streep

Chapter 1
The Perfectionist

I f you have a keen eye for detail, are a good planner who sees things through to completion, and like things to be correct, there is a strong chance you are a Type 1 personality—The Perfectionist. Some may also refer to this person as a reformer or idealist. Perfectionists have received a bad reputation because of their "everything has to be right" energy. They focus on doing a good job, providing great quality, and being right. Much of their attention is spent on figuring out what is wrong and how they can improve a thing or situation. This type of person may seem critical and judgmental to many, but it's only because they want to ensure that everything within their control is as close to perfect as possible. Type 1s are in constant self-monitoring mode. They are very much in control of themselves and like to control their environment. Not only are they critical of others, but they can also be very critical of themselves.

Type 1s have a high personal standard for behavior and performance. They are well organized, and it bears repeating that they have an extremely good eye for detail. They can spot an error in a newspaper a hundred miles away. Perfectionists are highly responsible, heavy on fairness, and extremely honest—sometimes to their own detriment.

Type 1s make great leaders. They like consistency and fairness; equity and justice are very important to them. Perfectionists are very conscientious and aim to always do a good job. They are quite dutiful; they lead by example and strive for high quality. If you work with a Type 1, you need to know they have high expectations regarding quality and are not fond of mediocracy. They commit to finishing the job and meeting your expectations, often going above and beyond. When expressing your expectations, you must make them clear. As well, they will not hesitate to make their expectations known.

Type 1s often have difficulty delegating. The story they tell themselves is that they are the only ones who can do the job in the way that is required. Being under the thumb of management can be difficult for Type 1s because they have certain standards that others may not have. They have to be okay with someone not working as long or as hard as them and accept that the person may not do the job the way they would. In other words, their high standards and expectations may not be shared by all. Type 1s have a hard time silencing their inner critic. They don't like making mistakes and can be hard on themselves. So, if you know someone with a Type 1 personality, take it easy on them. Trust me, they have probably already beaten themselves up enough.

Type 1s approach their work more seriously than the other personality types. Type 1s would do themselves well if they could ease up from their internal criticizing and recognize that the 80/20 rule is okay, accepting that 80% is good enough. Everything doesn't always have to be 100%.

Type 1s' inner critic leads to many issues. They can do or say something, then reflect on it and be extremely critical of themselves. It's almost as though they have a little voice in their head that is always gnawing away with its inner dialogue of critical comments, which can lead them to feel disappointed in themselves or constantly let down. Their expectations of themselves—and sometimes of others—can be a little overwhelming and overpowering. Type 1s can become engulfed in the details, and as a result, they end up not being as productive as they would like. In turn, their lack of productivity causes them to feel guilty, and they start focusing even harder on getting the task done, delaying pleasurable experiences and sacrificing time with their family and friends.

Sadly, Type 1s have a difficult time relaxing and just being. They feel many imperatives pushed on them by their personality type. What happens if they allow themselves to be consumed by that critical inner voice? They can become so consumed with getting things right that the overall task and importance can be lost. In some cases, they may not accomplish what they are so good at doing—finishing on time and within budget. They feel a strong obligation to deliver and experience guilt if they don't deliver at a perfect standard. The stress from their need to be perfect can be physically taxing, resulting in tension in their body.

Type 1s are burdened by their sense of personal responsibility for every aspect of their lives. They can feel overburdened by thinking they need to be the one to fix everything wrong. They get stressed when other people around them are not acting responsibly or performing to the high standard of Type 1. Failing to achieve perfection in whatever they do also makes them feel stressed. One of the biggest stressors for Type 1 personalities is that they think they must control everything to ensure it is done promptly and without error. Of course, we know nothing is perfect, and we can't control everything in our lives, but try convincing a perfectionist of this logic. Type 1s could do themselves some good if they learned to recognize and manage the impulses that result in them being in a hyper state, feeling they must be in control of every aspect of their lives and others.

Not taking criticism personally would be a really good start for Type 1s to lessen their desire to always achieve perfection. They are just as hard on themselves as they are on others. They think about the intent—for things to be as good as they can be. Again, they become stressed when they feel overwhelmed, so be clear about the expectations and don't overload them with tasks— because they will want to complete those tasks on time and at a very high standard. If they fail at doing that, they will be terribly self-critical.

When under stress, Type 1s can show some Type 4 tendencies, where they get more emotional and creative. Sometimes they can feel misunderstood or alone; that's when their frustration starts to show. In a relaxed state (which may not seem to occur often), Type 1s are more spontaneous, especially when rules and responsibilities are not binding them. These are the times when they can fully enjoy the moment.

Learning to let things go is one of the best things any Type 1 person can do. LET. IT. GO. This is challenging for perfectionists, though. Unless they're not paying attention to what's happening around them, which is rare, they won't recognize the need to let something go because they'll already be drowning in self-criticism, self-judgment, or judging somebody else in a critical way.

I recently worked with a very talented actress who I believe was a Type 1, but I didn't know it at the time. She was meticulous, wanting everything to be perfect, but the dark side, it seemed, was that she tried to control her castmates and take over as director. She soon got overwhelmed trying to control everything and had an emotional breakdown, which brought all of our spirits down. Then this amazing production became more about making her happy—or at least functional—than us creating a beautiful story for the audience. Had I known then what I know now, I would have certainly had more empathy for her and understood that she just wanted the production to be great like we all did.

Once Type 1s make it a regular practice of paying attention to their thoughts, feelings, and behavior, they'll notice they are too critical of themselves and others. This is when they can choose to let some things go or at least partly. They need to practice being more tolerant and understanding towards themselves and others.

In Type 1's mind, there is always something they need to get done—*"I can't relax because I have housework to do." "I can't go out to have dinner because I have to finish this project."* They limit their opportunities to relax and have fun, often feeling guilty for even considering it. It would do them good if they practiced having a work-life balance. They need to force themselves to take time to relax.

Type 1s need to find the time in their busy schedules to exercise as a form of self-care. Getting massages on a regular basis is another fabulous stress reliever. Learning some form of mindfulness and practicing it regularly leads to greater awareness. When Type 1s are in a more aware state and faced with a challenge, they can recognize it and realize they need to chill out before they freak out—*pause, breathe, reflect.* Type 1s should adjust their mindset from being drawn to what is wrong (negatives) and start focusing on the things that are right (positives). Let it go. Let it go. Let. It. Go.

Shaunté Massard

Character Example of Type 1: The Perfectionist

An Overview of
THE AMEN CORNER by James Baldwin

Margaret Alexander, a female pastor of a storefront church in the 1960s, is greatly admired by her congregation. After her long-lost musician husband returns, Margaret struggles to keep the congregation's respect. She almost loses her leadership of the church when the congregation sees how she deals with her 'wicked' husband and her wayward son, David. In the end, her final reconciliation with her husband purges Margaret of bitterness and gives her the strength to continue her religious mission.

MARGARET: But, dearly beloved, she can't come to you—the world can't come to you—if you don't live holy. This way of holiness is a hard way. I know some of you think Sister Margaret's too hard on you. She don't want you to do this and she won't let you do that. Some of you say, "Aint no harm in reading the funny papers." But children, yes, there's harm in it. While you reading them funny papers, your mind ain't on the Lord. And if your mind ain't stayed on Him, every hour of the day, Satan's going to cause you to fall. Amen! Some of you say, "Ain't no harm in me working for a liquor company. I ain't going to be drinking the liquor. I'm just going to be driving the truck! But a saint of God ain't got no business delivering liquor to folks all day—how you going to spend all day helping folks into hell and then think you going to come here in the evening and help folks into heaven? It can't be done. The Word tells me, No man can serve two masters!

Chapter 2
The Helper

A re you a heartfelt and passionate person who supports and cares for others more than yourself (sometimes to the point of exhaustion)? If so, I'm sure you will have no trouble relating to this personality type, The Helper. Type 2 is incredible in their level of emotional intelligence. They are also known as the giver, the caregiver, the supporter, the enabler, or the nurturer. You can see from these names they bring out the essential nature of Enneagram 2.

Type 2s are strong, assertive, and passionate, particularly about things they believe in. This personality type is also extremely generous and helpful, and they tend to be driven by their need to meet the needs of "important" others. Gaining approval and acceptance from "important" others helps them to feel good about themselves; it's how they earn much of their self-worth. Type 2s often change who they are to accommodate the "important" needs of the "important" people. Type 2s love being of service to others and fulfilling their needs—and again, especially for those they consider "important" to them.

As you can see, "important" is the keyword here. It is not that they disregard or have no disrespect for the average Joe, but their focus is on those who they deem important, such as leaders in the community, church, or social settings. They tend to gravitate towards people in power.

This personality type is compassionate, expressive, empathetic, and overly generous, which makes them great friends to have. They usually have a radar that is good for picking up on when someone is going through something emotionally. When they encounter someone suffering emotionally, their impulse is to help them in whatever way possible.

Because of their big hearts, they can become overly

emotional, particularly regarding injustice, lack of equity, or fairness. They intend to build relationships, great communicate well, and bring people together. As a leader or manager, they like empowering the people—wanting to bring out the best in them. Type 2s prefer relationship-oriented leadership so they can see their staff as people with a common goal. They could improve in their leadership role if they practiced saying no. However, because of their impulsive personality to care for, nurture, and support, denying others is often not easy for them to do.

They have the impulse to take on too many things that they may not have the resources or energy to take on. They often get exhausted. So, learning to prioritize and say no, particularly to things that aren't necessarily part of what they should be doing, would benefit their mental and emotional health. A good start would be encouraging others to be less dependent on them and getting people to make their own decisions instead of "wanting" people to refer to them. They should bring more objectivity, but because their personality drives them, they have a problem saying no—always being a people-pleaser. Sometimes they can be too accommodating for their own good.

If Type 2s make the mistake of not focusing enough on themselves, it will cause them to lose touch with what they need in their personal life. This can lead to them experiencing a sense of loss, rejection, and feeling vulnerable. When they don't receive a payoff in the form of a smile, acknowledgement, or praise from a partner or boss, they start to feel unappreciated, disregarded, or disrespected, which can lead to anger or resentment.

Type 2s take pride in being loving, caring, and kind. However, they tend to flatter other people too much and can almost behave like a martyr sometimes. Having invested so much of themselves in others, Type 2s may find that things of importance to them are often left undone. There is a limit, but they seldom know what that limit is for them, which results in them becoming worn out emotionally. Those people in the lives of Type 2s should set limits on how much they allow Type 2s to do for them because they will just keep giving.

I have a Type 2 who is very near and dear to my heart. He is everybody's best friend. Every friend he makes is for a lifetime. He is extremely giving of his time, energy, and resources at church, work, and home. He can usually be found very close to the person in charge, being of assistance in some form or fashion. The downside is that he has no boundaries. He gets calls and texts, day in and day out, and is attentive to every single one. He has made himself the "go-to" person in every setting, but on the flip side, he doesn't choose to ask for help. For the most part, he can juggle his high-paying job and beloved church family well, even when there are "fires" to put out, but when it comes to his home life, he often puts things on the back burner and even neglects himself emotionally. When overwhelmed and exhausted, he explodes and tries to ask for help, but by then, the emotional damage is already done to those "important" relationships in his personal life.

Type 2s move to Type 8 (The Challenger) when they are more assertive and display quick emotional anger. When in a relaxed state, Type 2s move to Type 4 (The Individualist), and that's when their creative side shines through.

This personality type is giving, but why? They should ask themselves if the reason they are so giving is for others (selfless) or themselves (selfish). They should identify needs and their identity in relationships with "important" people. Some things a Type 2 can do to get back to self is to get a massage or go for a walk. When they nurture self, they can be a selfless giver. However, if all their focus is on fulfilling the needs of others, they will exhaust themselves. Take a timeout and ask yourself what you need to do for yourself right now. If not, you will struggle with giving too much. Get into the practice of saying no and thinking about yourself first.

Shaunté Massard

Character Example of Type 2: The Helper

An Overview of
FENCES by August Wilson

Briefly, August Wilson's play *Fences* tells the story of Troy Maxson, an African American garbage collector and ex-convict who once had a promising future in baseball. His circumstances as a youth led him to prison, after which he settled down with Rose and made a family.

Rose exemplifies the traits of a Type 2. She puts her family first and supports her husband and son with compassion and hope while not begrudging their present stagnant situation.

Finding You in Every Script

ROSE: I been standing with you! I been right here with you, Troy. I got a life too. I gave eighteen years of my life to stand in the same spot with you. Don't you think I ever wanted other things? Don't you think I had dreams and hopes? What about my life? What about me? Don't you think it ever crossed my mind to want to know other men? That I wanted to lay up somewhere and forget about my responsibilities? That I wanted someone to make me laugh so I could feel good? You not the only one who's got wants and needs. But I held on to you, Troy. I took all my feelings, my wants and needs, my dreams…and I buried them inside you. I planted a seed and watched and prayed over it. I planted myself inside you and waited to bloom. And it didn't take me no eighteen years to find out the soil was hard and rocky and it wasn't never going to bloom. But I held on to you, Troy. I held you tighter. You was my husband. I owed you everything I had. Every part of me I could find to give you. And upstairs in that room…with the darkness falling in on me…I gave everything I had to try and erase the doubt that you wasn't the finest man in the world. And wherever you was going…I wanted to be there with you. Cause you was my husband. Cause that's the only way I was going to survive as your wife. You always

Shaunté Massard

talking about what you give…and what you
don't have to give. But you take, too. You
take…and don't even know nobody's giving!

Chapter 3
The Achiever

WHEN IS THE HOUSE TOUR COMING?

Type 3, The Achiever, is a go-getter who—like their name–seeks to achieve. They are goal-oriented and strive to be the best in whatever they do.

Sometimes called the performer, producer, succeeder, or initiator, these people live in the "Just Do It" Nike zone. Type 3s are efficient, effective, and very productive. Their competitive nature makes this individual someone you can count on to deliver. Type 3s are quite sensitive to the image they project and are good at "faking it 'til they make it," giving a false impression of confidence. They are highly motivated, have high emotional intelligence, and feel good about getting things done. They are quite adaptable to whatever context they are working in. As a result, they find it very easy to conform to the circumstance in order to achieve their goals. If they fall short of accomplishing what they set out to do, which is rare, they can be very hard on themselves, acting as if they created the greatest sin by failing to meet or exceed their goal. Type 3 are intolerant of things and people who get in their way; they become impatient or insensitive if they are prevented from achieving their goals.

Type 3s are task-oriented. Most write out a list of the things they need to accomplish, and some have the list stored in their mind. When they get something done and cross it off the list, it supercharges them to get even more done. They thrive on positive feedback and gaining others' approval. Winning, accomplishing, and succeeding are the things that drive them. They tend to do whatever is needed to reach the end goal quickly and efficiently. They are great at managing their time and staying within budget. When failure happens, it can be devastating for a Type 3, but they are usually able to deal with it and will work hard to minimize future errors. Type 3's are workaholics. They have a "can-do" attitude and are always looking for the most efficient way to do something.

Type 3 bosses are multitaskers and sometimes take shortcuts. They are more inclined to reward staff for competence and efficiency. They are optimistic, inspirational, and can be entrepreneurial. They may come across as confident, but that can be a veneer. Type 3s can be great project planners. However, they can improve on this by relating to the people instead of strictly focusing on tasks, toning down their competitiveness, and being truthful about who they are instead of hiding behind an illusion of greatness.

Type 3s desire to be the best in *every* area of their lives––work, sports, etc. Their competitiveness and drive to hit goals lead to them not having much time to reflect. They don't make time to focus on their relationship with others or themselves. They ignore their personal feelings, and as a result, they lose touch with the elements needed for a healthy relationship with others. They can be abrupt, blunt, or show impatience with others, especially those they perceive as holding them back from achieving their goals.

They are always aware of how they are coming across to other people. Using their emotional intelligence, they filter how their words and body language affect other people and will change themselves accordingly to do what they believe is necessary to hit their goals. But they should work on not putting on a persona because sometimes it can lead to them not being viewed as geniune or authentic, which could negatively affect their relationships with other people. Their intense drive to achieve can put people off at times.

Type 3s ignore their deepest feelings when focused on completing a task; however, when they finish, that's when they connect to their own emotions and the emotions of others around them. The Type 3s of the world need to recognize that they are not what they do but a beautiful essence of a being, and they need to connect with that essence regularly. Type 3s can become stressed juggling a lot of balls. If there is too much on their plate, they will be stressed that it won't all get done, and they won't receive the approval they desire. At the core, it's all about getting approval. Not knowing their feelings or feeling insecure can also lead to them experiencing stress. Type 3s need a better work-life balance and to learn to put things into perspective.

Type 3s can exhibit traits of Type 9, becoming indecisive when too much is going on and not being productive. When relaxed, Type 3s can go to Type 6 and become more thoughtful, more grounded, and make more time for reflection.

A friend of mine is what I believe is a Type 3, and he always gets the job done. He runs the video and audio equipment, creates graphic designs for the logos and tshirts, sets up the social media platforms, ministers regularly, and takes care of his body through exercise and nutrition. He even wears Nike "Just Do It" gear. He has impeccable style, wants nothing but the best, and has the perfect family—a beautiful wife and 2.5 kids. We all want to be "like Mike". Then there have been moments where the "mask" came off. He was vulnerable and transparent through sharing his troubled past, which allowed us all to know that we are human and, therefore, it is okay to be flawed.

Type 3s should allow others to see the real self behind their mask. They have to stop, reflect, and meditate so they can come back to themselves. If not, they will crash and burn. Type 3s need to do like India Arie says: "Slow down baby, you're going too fast." Then they can be their authentic self.

Character Example of Type 3: The Achiever

An Overview of
DREAMGIRLS by Tom Eyen and Henry Krieger

Deena, Effie, and Lorrell form a teenage music trio called the Dreamettes. When ambitious manager Curtis Taylor Jr. spots the act at a talent show, he offers the chance of a lifetime, to be backup singers for a national star, Jimmy Early. Taylor takes creative control of the group and eventually pushes the singers into the spotlight. However, one becomes the star, forcing another out, which teaches them about the high cost of fame.

Jimmy Early, the sexy, charismatic, high-energy, and married performer who is reminiscent of James Brown, exhibits the traits of a Type 3.

Finding You in Every Script

(JIMMY enters the dressing room)

C.C.
Mr. Early, you were great!

JIMMY
Thank you. Thank you. Thank you. It ain't
working, Marty. Man, I remember when that
faint, it used to kill 'em!

MARTY
Used to kill 'em, didn't it?

JIMMY
They used to lay down in
the aisles, baby.

MARTY
Yes, they did.

JIMMY
Too many other people doin' it now.

MARTY
Yeah, Jimmy, everybody's doin' it now.

JIMMY
And I was the first! You know that, don't
you.

Shaunté Massard

MARTY

And you're still the first, Jimmy, you're
still the first. You killed 'em tonight.
It was beautiful. Beautiful!

JIMMY

You're full of shit, Marty.
You know that?
You are full of shit. I told you, man,
I need new material.

(A girl passes)

Like that! Lord have mercy! Mama!

CURTIS

Jimmy, I want you to meet this young man…

C.C.

Claridge Conrad White.
I'm the writer for the Dreamettes.

JIMMY

Oh, yeah. You wrote that song those
little girls did out there.
How'd that go?
It went something like YOU BETTER MOVE.
You wrote that one, huh?

Finding You in Every Script

C.C.
Totally alone with absolutely
no help from anyone.

JIMMY
What do you think, Marty?

MARTY
Well, I think it's kind of…kind of…

JIMMY
Boring.

MARTY
Yeah. It's real boring, kid.

C.C.
I'm no kid, mister.

CURTIS
This is a very talented composer.

JIMMY
That's probably true but the song
just didn't have enough soul in it.
You know what I mean, brother?
Look, I'm Jimmy and I gotta have soul.
I gotta have soul, baby!

Chapter 4
The Individualist

Are you a creative, sensitive to the feelings of self and others, and sometimes find yourself riding a roller coaster of emotions? If so, chances are you are a Type 4, The Individualist. They are also called the artist, the romantic, the "tragic" romantic, and the the aesthetic.

A Type 4s' key goal is authenticity—being true to themselves. The attributes of Type 4s are they are deeply emotional and sensitive. These personality traits cause them to feel different from other people—special, unique. Type 4s focus on inner feelings, creating highs and lows for themselves. They can go from elation to sadness, all within the span of a minute. Type 4 tends to live their life in a constant search for what is special, different, and unique. It's almost as if they seek anything but the ordinary.

Type 4s are the most creative out of the other personality types. In addition to being creative, they are emotionally intelligent and sensitive beings. They are very attuned to their feelings and the feelings of others, and they do not hesitate to help others.

Type 4s give a lot of attention to their staff when in a managerial role and seek meaning through those interpersonal connections. They are relational, inspiring, and quite intuitive about the feelings of their team. Type 4s can improve by reducing the intensity and drama in relationships and the workplace, focusing more on the positives.

Because of their high level of sensitivity, Type 4s can experience a roller coaster of feelings—high highs and low lows, sometimes misinterpreting someone's look or a spoken word. They create challenges by their deep feelings fluctuating. Type 4s should find balance and work on keeping their emotions in check. They will learn their personality by taking the time to observe themselves. This will allow them to pause and reflect on what's happening and then respond appropriately. If not, they will always believe "the grass is greener on the other side," which will generate envy and sadness.

Type 4s are one of the idealist types. Their personality helps manifest an idealized world of love, authenticity, and creativity. At times, it can be difficult for a Type 4 to cope in a world that is flawed and not ideal. Type 4s will display outpours of anger, aggression, and judgement. They may even feel dissatisfied and disappointed with themselves and others.

Their personality always causes them to feel different, but they don't have a problem with this because Type 4s value uniqueness. When they live in a fantasy world and create a romantic relationship with someone who they believe is their ideal mate, it can be very disappointing for them if it doesn't manifest that way. They have mood shifts that can be intense and quick. Type 4s become stressed when people or experiences don't live up to their self-created romantic ideas or desire for intensity. Type 4s can experience feelings of rejection when people let them down. People not being authentic with them can cause them to display anger through dramatic outbursts or even bring on a depressed state. They should acknowledge and recognize their feelings of sensitivity and empathy.

It would be valuable to any workplace to let Type 4s express themselves creatively. Type 4s want the opportunity to be extraordinary. When under pressure, Type 4s show the

Type 2 trait—hardened submission. In a relaxed state, Type 4s can go to being a Type 8, The Challenger—productive, organized, and getting things done.

Full disclosure: I am a Type 4 through and through. I have always considered myself the "black sheep" of my family. I have always had big dreams, not wanting to settle for the status quo. I have moved from state to state and traveled the world, finally settling in California to pursue a new life in the entertainment industry. Although my chosen profession is acting, I didn't think I was an emotional person in real life. That's because I didn't allow my true self to come out of my shell often. My marriage has taught me a lot about myself— how I tend to focus on what I want to see instead of what is. I am sensitive to energy, not just words and actions. Recently, I opened myself up to forming friendships with new people, especially women, and found myself going through that roller coaster of emotions I mentioned earlier. I was in search of authentic friends who are caring, supportive, ambitious (but not competitive), funny (but not mean in humor), and spiritually, physically, and mentally healthy. Through this process, I got my feelings hurt, and I admit I was judgemental at times. However, now, I have what I was searching for—a healthy circle of beautiful, creative beings like me. Type 4s are deeply emotional individuals and should be grateful for what they have rather than brooding over what they do not have. Type 4s should put their focus on tangible things and their actions towards achieving real goals. Type 4s also focus on the full blossom of creativity and appreciate the ordinary. Practicing gratitude is immensely important for Type 4s. You should always have an attitude of gratitude.

Shaunté Massard

Character Example of Type 4: The Individualist

An Overview of
PARADISE BLUE by Dominique Morisseau

Blue, a gifted trumpeter, contemplates selling his once-vibrant jazz club in Detroit's Blackbottom neighborhood to shake free the demons of his past and better his life. But where does that leave his devoted Pumpkin, who has dreams of her own? And what does it mean for the club's resident bebop band? When a mysterious woman, Silver, with a walk that drives men mad comes to town with her own plans, everyone's world is turned upside down. This dynamic and musically-infused drama shines light on the challenges of building a better future on the foundation of what our predecessors have left us.

Silver is a sexy, charming, and spicy woman—gritty and raw in a way that men find irresistible. She shot and killed her husband. She can't have babies. She has a meeeeeaaaannnn walk. Silver is definitely a Type 4.

Finding You in Every Script

SILVER
I know you been through my things.

(PUMPKIN freezes for a second, and then quickly enters the room—closing the door behind her.)

PUMPKIN
It was only an accident—

SILVER
'Course it was.

PUMPKIN
I didn't mean to be inconsiderate.
I just came to change the sheets—

SILVER
And listen to a little Lester Young and
sort through my drawers.

PUMPKIN
I didn't—

SILVER
Relax, honey. No need to worry so.
I ain't mad at you.

PUMPKIN
It was a terrible mistake
and I swear I won't do it again.

SILVER
You see somethin' you like?
Want it for ya'self?

PUMPKIN
Oh, no, Missus. No, I don't want to
bother in any more of your things.

SILVER
You sho?

PUMPKIN
Yes, ma'am.

SILVER
Cuz I figure you musta got a lil' curious
'bout something. And I can take all
that curiosity away right now.

PUMPKIN
No, I'm fine. Really.

SILVER
Just let you have a lil' look-see.

(SILVER pulls out the gun. It shines in
the light. PUMPKIN gasps.)

This what you so 'fraid of?
This lil' bitty thing?

PUMPKIN
(Nervously) I...I don't need to see that,
Missus. It's your...private—

SILVER
Ain't too private no more. Or is it?
You tell me.

PUMPKIN
I ain't...told nobody...

SILVER
No? Not even yo' man?

PUMPKIN
No...nobody...

SILVER
Hunh... *(Pause.)* Well, that's good then.
Men find out a woman got a gun, they
ready to lock her in a dungeon and throw
away the key.

PUMPKIN
Why you...why you have it?

SILVER
For protection.

PUMPKIN
Protection from who?

SILVER
Anybody. Everybody. You think a woman can move on her lonesome from town to town without the know-how to put a bullet in somebody's head?

PUMPKIN
That ain't for a lady to do.

SILVER
Says who?

PUMPKIN
That's why a woman ain't supposed to be on her lonesome. Travel with a man by your side and he be all the protection you need.

SILVER
That so? That what your man do for you? Make you feel protected and safe?

PUMPKIN
'Course he does.

SILVER
That's why you got those bruises on your arm? Seems to me like you ain't no safer than me on my lonesome. In fact, I'll say I'm the better of us two. Cuz I know how to shoot straight and aim direct. And I

ain't shy when I got this in my hand, neither. Ain't no wallflower. I'm front and center on the floor. And I ain't afraid to use it. That's where people get you. They see you got it but don't 'spect you to use it. But once somebody see yo' gun, they done seen all your cards right there on the table. So you either fold, or you take the win. And me, I always take the win.

PUMPKIN
What happened to yo' husband?

SILVER
That's a tale for another day.

PUMPKIN
Why you move here on your lonesome?

SILVER
I told you, he died.

PUMPKIN
How he die?

SILVER
Bullet in the head.

Chapter 5
The Observer

Type 5 is intensely private, analytical, emotionally detached, and often plays an observer role. This personality type is also known as the analyst, the thinker, the philosopher, the sage, the investigator, or the recluse. Type 5s key goal is seeking knowledge, retaining knowledge, and using that knowledge in any way they like. The key factor of Type 5s is detachment from their feelings and others, and they are good at rational, logical thinking. Type 5s like to take an objective approach to everything; however, they can be hypersensitive. Type 5s are deep thinkers and possess deep layers of knowledge, especially if a subject matter interests them. When they do their analysis, they look at things from all angles.

Most Type 5s are procrastinators. They focus on reducing feelings, reducing needs, not using a lot of resources, and can get by in a minimalist way. Type 5s tend to compartmentalize everything in their lives. They have friends for every setting—school friends, work friends, church friends. Everything and everybody is organized in a file in their mind. Type 5s do not like high emotions being thrown at them by others. It can be quite disturbing and cause them to go into their "cave"; it might be a physical cave or one that they created in their mind.

Accumulation of knowledge is hugely important. Knowledge is like a suit of armor to defend themselves from the attacks of the outside world. The gifts of Type 5 are being objective, analytical, thoughtful, and reflective. Their greatest gift is that they are strong, independent thinkers. They are incredibly clever, particularly in areas of their expertise.

Type 5s make good managers and are systematic in their planning. Persistent and strong, they can work through things in a very calm and objective way. When challenges arise, they like to think things through. Type 5s tend to think analytically and gather information. Therefore, they will take the time to analyze and reflect before giving you an answer. So, don't expect to just bounce into their office and get an answer straight away. They want to make an informed decision based on data. Type 5s can improve by focusing on the action and analysis, thereby lessening procrastination. Type 5s may face challenges as a manager in regards to their relationship with a volatile team with high emotions. Type 5s should focus on understanding the feelings of the people they are looking after. Taking action is a big step for Type 5s, as there can be paralysis by analysis. They should recognize when they have enough information to make a decision and move forward.

Type 5s are all about knowledge, self-sufficiency, and self-dependency. They don't like being told anything, even if they need to be told.

They tend to shy away from emotional relationships. Yet, if they open themselves up to a world of emotions, they open themselves to a degree of rich connections and love. Type 5s aloof demeanor can cause challenges in relationships. Unfortunately, they have a tendency to ignore not only their feelings but the feelings of other people around them, which leads to problems in their relationships. In business relationships, it is problematic and leads to teams not functioning anywhere near their potential.

Type 5s' incredibly independent nature makes them believe they can function without any support or guidance from others. Sometimes it may work for them, but they need input from other people a lot of the time. Their personality pushes Type 5s to underemphasize the power of relationships and connections. They can become miserable when having to share information, deal with emotions, and make connections with others. Their intense desire for privacy applies to every aspect of their lives; they don't want or welcome intrusions into their private space. Type 5s can get angry, withdraw, and not communicate when people place demands on them. It makes them want to disappear.

Type 5s are usually reserved, so they are not likely to boast about their expertise or toot their own horn. If you want to know something, you may need to just ask, as they are not very forthcoming with information. They will usually be happy to impart their knowledge, but only on their terms. Spontaneous meetings don't work for Type 5s; they want to have the time to prepare in advance. Type 5s can be in a better relationship with their computer and email than with people. They could use help in the workplace—and even places outside of their job—to get in touch with their feelings.

Allow Type 5s to start out in their observer role so they

can collect their thoughts and then ask them what they can add to the conversation. When under stress, Type 5s share traits with Type 7, The Optimist, meaning they can have a lot going on but not getting anything done and acting as if nothing is that serious. In a relaxed state, Type 5s go to Type 8—less thinking, more action, and getting things done. Type 5s can improve by paying more attention to their feelings and the feelings of those around them. Type 5s also need to pay attention to their physical well-being by moving and exercising their bodies since most of their activity seems to only happen in their mind.

Wow! There has never been a truer statement that describes another loved one of mine who I shall not name. I'll just refer to him by the nickname we call him, which is Kung Fu Panda. He is quite a fluffy, teddy bear-like young man who can literally stay in his "cave" and hibernate for days or even months at a time. He doesn't interact much with anyone during that time, only coming out to seek his true love—food. He also has a very fond relationship with his computer, cell phone, and TV. It seems he feels more comfortable with screens than actual humans, mainly because he can gather loads of information online and on TV. It is fascinating what he knows, how much he knows, and who he knows from watching and listening to YouTubers and bloggers. Being that we are living in the informational age, having this type of access to everything is a dream come true for him. He gathers this knowledge without any real purpose for having it other than to offer what he has learned in casual conversation, without any plans to form a bond from his interaction with others. Yet, he is one of the most thoughtful and caring people I know.

Type 5s need to actively practice generosity in every aspect of their being—not only generosity with their data, information, and insight but also generosity of their spirit and love with other people. Less compartmentalizing. Instead, allow people in and connect in their lives. Try to live spontaneously rather than limit themselves in the way they normally live their lives. By them being more spontaneous, they give more value to their relationship and connection with important people. Type 5s need to allow people into their "cave". They should practice being more connected, expressing their feelings more openly, and increasing their capacity to engage rather than withdraw. Again, pay more attention to your feelings and the feelings of others.

Character Example of Type 5: The Observer

An Overview of
THE TALENTED TENTH by Richard Wesley

The Talented Tenth spans the life and career of Bernard Evans, a successful African American radio executive whose midlife crisis has reached critical mass. A civil rights activist and Howard University graduate, Bernard settled into a comfortable life and reaped the benefits of a professional career, enjoying a state of prosperity and power. But something is missing, and Bernard is determined to reclaim the part of his life he feels he has lost.

Bernard exhibits Type 5 personality traits.

(Pam and Bernard are having breakfast. She looks through the mail.)

BERNARD
I'm thinking about going out to the stadium to see the ball game. Want to come?

PAM
Baseball?

BERNARD
Yea.

PAM
Can I think about it?

BERNARD
Sure…

(He continues eating. She looks through the mail. BERNARD looks at her.)

Anything interesting?

PAM
Just the usual bills…junk mail…

(Looks at Bernard.)

I ran into Sylvia Witherspoon, yesterday.

BERNARD
How's she doing?

PAM
She told me you and her husband had
a fight at the station.

BERNARD
It was an argument. Not a fight.

PAM
She said you've been arguing a lot,
lately.

BERNARD
There are things I want to do, but can't.
He's one of the reasons I can't.

PAM
Is there anyone there you're
not fighting with?

BERNARD
Lots of people.

PAM
Bernard?

BERNARD
I had a nice time at the
fundraiser last night.

PAM

No, you didn't have a nice time. You danced and talked. But you never really said anything to anyone. You did it all night. And, just now, to me. You're effecting a conversation in order to avoid having a real one.

BERNARD

Aw, Pam, come on…

PAM

Silences, changes the subject; empty jokes. All means of keeping people away from you. Everyone likes who they think is you. The dedicated ex-boy wonder who always seems on top of everything. But, I was thinking that, after fifteen years of marriage, I still don't even know what your favorite color is.

BERNARD

You never asked.

PAM

You never told me.

BERNARD

Dark blue. What's yours?

Finding You in Every Script

PAM
Pink.

BERNARD
I thought it was yellow.

PAM
It's pink.

BERNARD
I could have sworn it was yellow.

PAM
Pink.

BERNARD
You never even wear pink.
Your favorite dress is yellow.

PAM
You see, you're doing it again.

BERNARD
Well, I'll be damned. Pink.

PAM
Bernard, I'm not just talking about pink
or yellow or dark blue. Ron noticed it,
too.

BERNARD

My alleged distance, I suppose.

PAM

Yes. We were talking.

BERNARD

You were talking about me?

PAM

After all these years he was surprised
about how little he knew about you.

BERNARD

You were talking to Ron about me.

PAM

Yes. He's your friend, Bernard.

BERNARD

(Sarcastic.) So he is.

PAM

What's that supposed to mean?

BERNARD

Ron can get to be a bit much, Pam.

PAM

He's a success at what he does. He's
happy, Bernard. So few of our people get

the kinds of opportunities he's getting.
Be glad for him. He's happy for us.

BERNARD
So, how about it?

PAM
What?

BERNARD
You want to go to the ball game with me?

Chapter 6
The Skeptic

YOU DON'T HAVE ANY IDEA
HOW MY TIRE GOT A FLAT, DO YOU?

T ype 6, The Skeptic, is an overthinker, may have self-doubt, and will doubt others. They tend to procrastinate and spend a lot of time thinking about what might go wrong. Type 6s are also called the questioner, the devil's advocate, the trooper, and the strategist. They have brilliant minds and are very clever.

One flaw of their personality is they doubt themselves and doubt what is presented to them. There is a level of mistrust, which creates anxiety where they find themselves constantly checking their environment, expecting something to go wrong. They are the worriers—the specialist in worry and anxiety.

Type 6s are the best risk managers on the whole because of their intense focus on safety and security. They are also clever and have analytical abilities. They like to work out what's happening, look at things every which way, and even sometimes check in with others. Their high-powered thinking has a cost. They do way more thinking than action, which causes them to procrastinate.

Type 6s are loyal, protective, warm, and insightful. They are often very witty and use humor as a defense mechanism. They are good problem finders and problem solvers. Type 6s can spot a hidden agenda; they have a radar if something's not quite right. They may be suspicious and doubt what they are told.

Type 6s are very loyal to companies, many working long-term for an organization. Their management style is based on trust, analysis, and security. They are efficient and responsible; they are strategic and have a sharp intellect. They can pick up on things before others and have the ability to anticipate and solve problems.

Type 6s can improve by working on curbing their anxieties through mindfulness (recognizing what causes them stress) and physical exercise (releasing stress). This personality type struggles with worry and weariness in every dimension of their lives. Their suspicion of everything, including themselves, causes them to experience much procrastination. They can catch themselves if they're not stepping into action and minimize procrastination. In relationships, they are very suspicious of those closest to them and will even question if the person still loves them. So, while they may be cautious regarding relationships, they can be loyal, warm, and loving. Be honest and open with them. Most importantly, keep your word.

As Type 6s go through their lives, they are always looking for danger; this causes them to be on alert constantly. They find it hard to relax, but it can be a beautiful thing when they find themselves in a relaxed space.

While in school, Type 6s will be the last to finish an assignment, a class project, or an exam. They feel they need to cover all the bases, so they will continue searching for information and data analysis until they are satisfied. When Type 6s are under the pressure of a deadline, they usually deliver, and when they finish, they typically do it brilliantly.

Type 6s don't like being attacked, and similar to Type 4s, they don't like inauthentic behavior. They want to be able to work things out for themselves. They don't like people who try to corner, control, or overly pressure them.

Shaunté Massard

For me, being in a relationship with a Type 6 was very challenging. I was in a long-term relationship with a young man who I believe was a Type 6, which started when I was right out of college. Not knowing his personality type (let alone not discovering my own until recently) led to many difficult circumstances and altercations. It's interesting that the Type 6s I know are attractive, charming, and have great smiles, so they are able to cover up that most times they are fearful and anxious with a smile or funny comment. They can come across as having it all together, but the dangerous thing is they can be suffering on the inside, and no one would know it. The lack of trust, transparency, and vulnerability in our relationship led to hurtful actions and feelings of being smothered and controlled. There was obviously a fear of our relationship ending, but the lack of trust caused even more problems, which created more distance between us and gave him exactly what he didn't want—an unhappily ever after ending. Knowing myself now as a Type 4, I believe if I had been more open and he more trusting, the outcome may have been different. Regardless of our ending, I hope for peace in his mind, body, and spirit.

Type 6s move to a Type 3, The Achiever, and will step into action when under pressure, like taking an exam or approaching a project deadline. Sometimes a Type 6 will step into action, finish the project, feel a sense of relief, but then immediately start having anxiety about the next big thing to do. That anxiety sits at a residual level all the time. Now, when they move into their relaxed state, they go to Type 9. This is when they get out of their mind and into their body and are less suspicious, more relaxed, and grounded.

Type 6 can improve by practicing mindfulness. Calmer activities can help in all dimensions of their lives. If they practice some form of mindfulness and start getting into action (exercising), they will be better able to manage the anxiety, self-doubt, and doubt of others. They will also find that they are more action-oriented, decisive, and productive.

They should take the time to do a reality check of their fears and worries. Quite often, these characteristics are amplified in the minds of Type 6s—way more than the other types. They are even known to be a bit hyper. However, if they learn about their personality type and become aware of their characteristics, they will handle uncomfortable and stressful situations better. Instead of worrying, procrastinating, or stressing over needing more information or doing an analysis, Type 6s will learn to relax, breathe, and then take action.

Another way for Type 6s to lessen their stress is to break down a long-term goal into mini goals—steps you take that will put you closer to achieving the end goal. Setting several target goals makes it easier for them to manage their lives and gauge their productivity. It also helps them to focus on the nearing date of the next goal rather than thinking they have plenty of time, which results in paralysis by analysis—realizing they don't have as much time as they thought. So, setting many goals is good for this personality type, and it also allows them to be more aware of their inner feelings. They operate so much thinking, analysis, and planning, often neglecting their feelings and not giving their bodies time to rest in a relaxed state.

Learning to trust is hard for every Type 6 on the planet. However, if they can put in place some of these strategies and trust in their abilities and others, they can be sensational performers, achievers, and incredible partners in relationships. Stop allowing yourself to be derailed because of your lack of trust in yourself and others. Ask yourself, "How much do I have to be concerned about the risk of this going wrong?" It's okay to already have a plan worked out in your head about certain scenarios: "If this happens or doesn't happen, I will do this, this, or this." Just don't become obsessed with expecting the worst in people or a situation. Shift your focus from thinking something will go wrong and start believing things will turn out right. You can begin by trusting others, but most importantly, learn to trust yourself.

Character Example of Type 6: The Skeptic

An Overview of
BOURBON ON THE BORDER by Pearle Cleage

After months at a mental rehabilitation hospital, Charlie returns home to his wife, May. He gets a job through Tyrone, the boyfriend of Rosa, May's best friend. Everything seems to be going fine for both of the couples. But it becomes clear that all of Charlie's problems were not solved during his time away. He must still face the traumatic events in his and May's past during the civil-rights movement, events that continue to creep into the present.

Charlie exemplifies the traits of a Type 6.

MAY
I told you not to go down there
in the first place.

CHARLIE
But not because you thought I was too
old. Because you thought I was too good,
so it's not like you get to say
I told you so.

MAY
I never say I told you so.

CHARLIE
Which is why I love you!
When are they coming?

MAY
Any minute now.

CHARLIE
Do I have time to change my shirt?

MAY
Sure.
(Charlie exits)
Charlie?

CHARLIE
Yeah?

MAY
Rosa said they might be hiring
on Tyrone's job.

CHARLIE
What job is that?

MAY
He drives a truck.

CHARLIE
Yeah? Local or long distance?

MAY
Local. You know I asked her that first!

CHARLIE
If I ever do another thing that makes
me have to leave your side for longer
than eight hours at a time, I want you to
do me a favor.

MAY
Anything.

CHARLIE
Shoot me.

MAY
Anything but that.

(The doorbell rings. May starts to answer, but Charlie stops her.)

CHARLIE
I got it.

(Charlie opens the door to Rosa and Tyrone.)

ROSA
Charlie Thompson!

(Rosa hugs Charlie warmly)

Welcome home, and meet Tyrone!
Ty, this is Charlie.

CHARLIE
Come on in.

TYRONE
Thanks, man. Good to meet you.

CHARLIE
Same here. How's it going, Rose?

ROSA
Same old, same old, but I can't complain.
MAY
Which doesn't mean she won't.
Hey, Tyrone.

Finding You in Every Script

TYRONE
Hey, May. Looking good, girl!

(Charlie has a visibly negative reaction to Tyrone's playful compliment. No one notices except May, who glances at Charlie nervously.)

ROSA
Do you have my silver hoops?

MAY
I think so.

ROSA
I need them for this dress, honey.
I'm naked without my earrings!
We'll be right back.

(Rosa pulls a slightly reluctant May into the bedroom)

TYRONE

(Looking after May admiringly)

You a lucky man, brother.

CHARLIE
That ain't something you got to tell me.

TYRONE

(Alerted by Charlie's tone.)

I didn't mean nothing by it.

CHARLIE

I didn't think you did. It just makes a
man feel funny when some other m!@#% is
as comfortable up in his house as he is.

TYRONE

It ain't like that, man. You can believe
it. Rosa and May are too tight for me to
be trying to even think something like
that. Besides, that woman loves you, man.
From what Rose says, she hardly left the
house since you been gone. Just sitting
around, waitin' on you. This is probably
only the third or fourth time
I've even seen her at all.

CHARLIE

No problem, man. Everything's cool.

(Charlie extends his hand. Tyrone shakes
it. Both are grateful that the bad moment
has passed.)

I've just been away, that's all.
Things can change.

Chapter 7
The Optimist

(LAUGHS)

Type 7 is The Optimist. They are also called the adventurer, the risk-taker, the epicure, the visionary, and the connoisseur. This personality type gets easily bored and distracted. They like a variety and interesting new places, people, and ideas. Their essence is fun and staying positive. The main attribute of Type 7 is being optimistic.

No matter their circumstances, part of Type 7s' nature

causes them to always look on the bright side. The bright side is way more fun. An element of their energy causes them to seek out positive experiences, activities, and pleasurable relationships. As they go about their lives, they are charming and inspiring to others; their positivity seems to infect others. People enjoy hanging out with Type 7s because of their Peter Pan energy—jumping from activity to activity and having fun. Of course, it's not always fun for Type 7s. If things in their life get dark or disappointing, the energy of Type 7 changes the focus of their attention from what is pleasant to facing what is wrong in their world. Stay positive while in the company of Type 7s, as negativity turns them off. They don't have a problem quickly removing themselves from anything or anyone negative.

Type 7s like stimulating and enjoyable experiences, whether alone or with others. It's interesting how they can be happy all by themselves on the back deck, having a drink while a party is going on inside with some of their closest friends. Type 7s are upbeat, engaging, spontaneous, and quite energetic, which makes people like to be around them. They often have a good sense of humor and a lovely optimism—the ability to connect the dots and see the possibilities. They can see a larger picture when others cannot. That's their innovation.

Type 7s can be risk-takers and have an entrepreneurial spirit. Their strengths are their ability to strategize, develop a plan, and follow through. They are quick-minded, avid learners, and driven by their curiosity. As leaders, they like to give people space to work things out for themselves. Type 7s are not micro-managers, nor do they like to be micro-managed. If you're working with a Type 7, tell them what you want, the outcome you desire, and then leave them be to work their way to it.

Type 7s move quickly. They are quick thinkers, often jumping in with a solution. It's good for Type 7s to make sure their people are keeping up with them because not everyone has a mind that moves as quickly as a Type 7. They should be mindful of this and slow their pace when necessary to allow people to catch up.

Type 7s can become highly offended if criticized, but if they step back and stop to think for a moment, they may find some truth in the criticism.

This personality type can be the most easily distracted and become bored very quickly. Type 7s need constant mental stimulation to feel okay. They like new experiences, interesting people, and intriguing ideas. It's nothing for them to be reading 3, 4, or 5 books at the same time or working on different projects simultaneously. Type 7s like to dance through the smorgasbord of everything life has to offer. For Type 7s, its about really prioritizing, completing, and doing what they said they would do.

Type 7s constant need for stimulation is a defense

mechanism because when they stop having something their mind is focused on, they can feel unnerved momentarily. It's almost as though they fear darkness is looming nearby and will cloak their personal or business relationships if they don't find something to fill the void. They would rather do anything—fishing, swimming, sailing, or anything else that is fun—than deal with the darkness.

Type 7s have an aversion to following rules because, in their mind, they like to have the freedom to work things out for themselves. Sometimes they make the mistake of moving too quickly on something without taking on enough advice or convincing their team it's the way to go. Intuitively, Type 7s already have the problem worked out in their head; they just aren't sure how to get to the solution.

The energy of Type 7s can become scattered. When that occurs, people think they are not being serious. However, Type 7s are always having a constant battle with their personality. They want to be able to do what they want to do when they want to do it. If they don't have freedom, they can feel trapped and become sad, dysfunctional, and angry at the world. In that situation, they're not the best leader, worker, partner, or even the best citizen. Type 7s like to have options, so if one door closes, there's another one that can open and soothe their senses. Then, they can direct their attention to what's more interesting or fun.

When in the role of a leader, Type 7s are responsible for doing what is required in the workplace and hitting their targets while leading their team with integrity. They need to be disciplined to do what needs to be done, and they need to do it by role modeling that behavior to their staff. They also need to truly listen to their staff. Type 7s tend to jump to conclusions or only think their way is the right way. When they don't actively listen to the people they work with, it can result in challenging relationships and poor outcomes. Type 7s can usually handle juggling many balls in the air. However, there are times when it will do them good to reevaluate their priorities and focus on finishing one thing at a time. They also need to make sure they are receptive and open to feedback. They need to open their hearts and minds to the fact that they might learn something that will serve them well in the future.

Commitment can be difficult for Type 7s, but once they commit, they can gain a lot of value from following through. Type 7s need clear contracts—either verbally or in writing—particularly in the workplace. They have a more flexible attitude regarding contracts than the rest of the world.

When under stress, Type 7s move to Type 1, The Perfectionist, giving more attention to detail and much more attention to finishing. There can be some rigidity that comes with this shift, including more self-control and making judgements if others aren't performing to their expectation. When relaxed, Type 7s move to Type 5, The Observer. This can be a much calmer place where they can be in their space alone and do some reflecting. Type 7s have a wonderful connection with the natural world. They can be in awe of the natural world when relaxing, so they become calmer and more analytical.

Type 7s can improve by recognizing that their compulsive pursuit of things can sometimes be excessive. They need to slow down their brains, tame their actions, and focus on one task at a time—getting that one thing done before moving on to the next. This may also help them to avoid scattered thinking and scattered actions. Type 7s should practice mindfulness—living in as many "now" moments as possible and cherishing those times. This will help them to become more self-aware and notice when their thinking is becoming too scattered so they can stop and redirect their focus to the real priorities.

Type 7s need to commit to important things, including relationships with others who they care about, both in their workplace and intimate relationships. By doing so, they will get the best out of themselves and those relationships. They certainly need to practice honoring their commitments. They need to open themselves up to not just skimming the surface of the smorgasbord of life but delving deeper to experience its richness, which sometimes includes dealing with life's challenging situations. The personality of Type 7 makes them turn their attention away from difficulties. But the reality is, if they want to move forward to success, they need to pause, head straight into it, and deal with it properly.

There is no doubt in my mind that one of my sweetest friends is a Type 7 because she is pure joy to be around. The first day we met, she walked up to me at a park with the biggest, brightest smile that I had ever seen and introduced herself. Ever since then, I have been drawn to her never-ending energy and positivity. She has such a big heart for people, especially those with physical, emotional, and mental disabilities; she dealt with her own disabilities in her life that she overcame through her faith. Her life's mission is to encourage other people who are struggling with spiritual, physical, and emotional paralysis to help them overcome and set them free.

Type 7s make the world an amazing place just by listening to other people, staying focused, and finishing what you start. By honoring your commitments, you become our superheroes.

Character Example of Type 7: The Optimist

An Overview of
A RAISIN IN THE SUN by Lorraine Hansberry

A Raisin in the Sun is the story of a lower-class African-American family, led by Mama Lena Younger, living on the Southside of Chicago during the 1950s. The family seeks to move into a home in a White middle-class neighborhood. Although a portion of a $10,000 insurance check has been used as a down payment on the house, the remainder of the money has been given to Walter Lee, the son of the family. In an effort to quadruple the money, he invests the money and ends up losing it all. Despite losing the remainder of the insurance money and being told they would not be welcome into the White neighborhood, the family decides to move forward with their plans to move into the new neighborhood with hopes for a bright future.

Walter Lee is a good example of a Type 7 personality.

MAMA

I'm sorry 'bout the liquor store, son. It just wasn't the thing for us to do. That's what I want to tell you about—

WALTER

I got to go out, Mama.

MAMA

It's dangerous, son.

WALTER

What's dangerous?

MAMA

When a man goes outside his home to look for peace.

WALTER

Then why can't there never be no peace in this house then?

MAMA

You done found it in some other house?

WALTER

No, there ain't no woman! Why women always think there's a woman somewhere when a man gets restless. Mama— — Mama— I want so many things…

Shaunté Massard

MAMA

Yes, son.

WALTER

I want so many things that they are
driving me kind of crazy… Mama, look at
me.

MAMA

I'm looking at you. You a good-looking
boy. You got a job, a nice wife, a fine
boy and——

WALTER

A job. Mama, a job? I open and close car
doors all day long. I drive a man around
in his limousine and I say, "Yes, sis;
no, sir; very good sir; shall I take the
drive, sir?"
Mama, that ain't no kind of job… that
ain't nothing at all. Mama, I don't know
if I can make you understand.

MAMA

Understand what, baby?

WALTER

Sometimes it's like I can see the future
stretched out in front of me—just plain
as day. The future, Mama. Hanging over
there at the edge of my days. Just

waiting for me——a big, looming blank space——full of nothing. Just waiting for me. *(Pause.)* Mama, sometimes when I'm downtown and I pass them cool, quiet-looking restaurants where them white boys are sitting back and talking 'bout things…sitting there turning deals worth millions of dollars…sometimes I see guys don't look much older than me——

MAMA
Son, how come you talk so much 'bout money?

WALTER
Because it is life, Mama!

Chapter 8
The Challenger

S trong. Determined. Gets things done. Big on honesty, fairness, and loyalty. These are the qualities of Type 8—the Challenger. Maybe you can relate to this personality type.

Type 8 is also called the boss, the protector, and the assertor. The key goal for someone who is a Type 8 is to be in control of themselves and their environment. They are good at committing and following things through. They can be direct, no-nonsense, and quite assertive. They are not afraid to stand up for their rights or for the rights of the people they care about. They go, go, go—sometimes to the point of being excessive. They are known to push the boundaries.

Type 8s are big on honesty, integrity, and justice. If they perceive someone is behaving unfairly or inappropriately towards them or someone they care about, their protective instincts will kick in. They will confront that person and let them know there could be some consequences for their actions.

Known for being the ones to get things done, Type 8s can become frustrated over someone else's procrastination or with people not doing what they are tasked to do. They are usually fully invested and committed to a particular task—whether work or play. They're great at organizing themselves, people, or other resources to make things happen. They can become quite frustrated, impatient, and even angry if held back.

Type 8s are very consistent with their words, which are powerful and courageous. They tend to only deal with those in their circle and are protective of their people. You're either in their circle or out, and understand that you must earn your place in their circle. Disloyalty is a deal-breaker for Type 8s. If you cross them or are dishonest, that can be a real issue.

It's "what you see is what you get" with Type 8s. They don't like games and are straight shooters. They are extremely self-sufficient, independent, decisive, and blunt––telling things how they are and not sugar-coating anything. It's not that they go looking for conflict; they just have the courage to sort things out when they need to be sorted out. Type 8s are confident assertive and will fight a good battle whenever necessary.

They are leaders and like to empower and develop others. Type 8s make great mentors and are always happy to support other people's successes. They move things forward, refusing to stay stagnant. They're energetic!

The Type 8 personality sees life as a fight against injustice, and they do not shy away from adversity. Achieving the goal of overcoming obstacles drives them.

Someone I can recall being a Type 8 personality is a woman I met at my church. Although the people within a spiritual community have different personalities, you unite through praise and worship music. Our worship leader is dynamic. She is strong and powerful in her delivery of songs about God being our protector, provider, and defender—attributes she also asserts in her relationships with others. Though relatively young physically and mentally, she is fondly called the "mother of the church." In addition to being the worship leader, she handles most of the church's business and relational matters. She is the go-to person for anything; if she doesn't know something, she will search to find out. She is bold yet submissive, doing whatever is necessary to accomplish the task at hand. She is a great asset to any family, community, project, or organization. Did I mention she can cook, too? That is one of the gifts she has that transforms this former group of riff-raff into believers living life together as a church family.

In a challenging situation, Type 8s are known to respond with anger. They could work on controlling their temper by pausing to reflect on the situation instead of being quick to react. They rarely consider opposite points of view or entertain the idea that there may be a different way of doing something.

Type 8s work hard and play hard, which can lead to them experiencing periods of exhaustion. They need to be more mindful of their energy because if they wear themselves out to the point of exhaustion, they're not going to be any good to themselves or anybody else.

They can sometimes take on a combative role in life or work. They see life as being in the midst of a battle, battling what—to them—are evil forces. Their energy is so big that when Type 8s walk in the room, there is a sense something is about to happen. They're strong and impressive beings when in a group of other people. However, they need to recognize that their impression of power and control can be perceived as unfavorable and make others fearful of them. Their body language can make them appear assertive or even aggressive, sometimes frightening people when that is not even their intention. They should be mindful of this when interacting with others.

There's an unconscious belief that Type 8s must always protect themselves. Also, they believe that they need to be self-sufficient and run their own race. The reality is, they have big hearts. They need to accept that they have big hearts and know it is okay to be vulnerable at times. Sometimes by being so controlling, they can derail relationships and their success. Sometimes, they put other people off by being overly demanding and pushing others to work or play as hard as they do. The expectation they put on themselves and others is sometimes unrealistic.

Those Type 8s who are good managers are great at empowering, training, and supporting their people. The not-so-good Type 8 managers sometimes push their staff so hard that some employees will leave the organization. They can often be blunt or tactless in how they deal with others.

Type 8s are stressed when people are unfair or behave in an unjust way. When someone does the wrong thing, that's a big trigger for Type 8, and they will respond in a firm and effective manner—sometimes taking a confrontational approach if necessary. Type 8 personalities reap justice on the perpetrators of injustice. Sometimes Type 8s cut people out of their lives. They need to do a reality check if that is the right path for them.

Type 8s like people who are honest, open, straightforward, and not afraid to tell them how it is. They will not hesitate to cut you out of their life if you prove not to be any of those things. They dislike those who avoid conflict with them and actually respect those who stay and face the music. However, when dealing with a Type 8, be cautious and don't take their anger or challenging nature personally when all they really want to do is sort things out. Despite their bold demeanor, Type 8s are surprised when somebody else finds them intimidating. You can help them tone down their intensity by getting them to realize they may get more out of people if they pull back a little and give themselves a chance to understand what's happening with the other person.

A Type 8s' traits can blend with Type 5: The Analyst when they're under pressure. This is when they quiet down a bit. They always say when a Type 8 gets quiet, look out. What they are doing is gathering information, developing a strategy, and in many ways withdrawing from a situation before coming back armed with information that will help their argument. A Type 8 is rarely able to be ambushed. When in a relaxed nature, they change to a Type 2: The Helper—picking up on the big heart, warmth, empathy, and nurturing energy of others.

Type 8s often will leap into action without giving much consideration to their feelings or the feelings of other people around them. They are sensational operators at that level, but sometimes they're so focused on taking action that they don't pause to consider and take advantage of the different personality styles. That will help them be better at every dimension of their existence. If they only allow themselves to be driven by their instincts, they will not have a broad enough spectrum of perspectives, which could help them to be the best they can be. They are powerful, but they also need to practice being gentle and understanding.

Type 8's should also prioritize care of themselves physically because they can become so engrossed in getting things done that they will neglect themselves in this area. They are a powerhouse, but sometimes they can wear their body out by all the stressors and demands they put themselves under. Regular exercise will do them good as well as learning to slow down. It's okay to allow others to be in control; however, this is not always easy for Type 8s. Vulnerability is big for a Type 8. They feel they must be strong and act as a defender or protector; therefore, it is rare for them to lower their defense mechanism and allow themselves to be vulnerable. If only a Type 8 could recognize that vulnerability is a strength, not a weakness, then greatness would ensue.

Finding You in Every Script

Character Example of Type 8: The Challenger

An Overview of
FLYIN' WEST by Pearle Cleage

Flyin' West is set in 1898 and follows a family of four black women—Sophie, Fannie, Minnie, and Ms. Leah—as they lay claim to land in Nicodemus, an all-black Kansas town. The play is a powerful commentary on sisterhood, identity, and race. It is based on the fact that in the late 19th century, many African Americans left the South to settle out West. Trouble starts when baby sister Minnie comes back into town from London with her mulatto new husband, Frank, to settle his slave-owner father's will.

Strong and tough, Sophie is fiercely loving and protective, and although she isn't related by blood, she is the head of the family that she has assembled. She is prepared to fight for her freedom, always armed with her shotgun and ready to point it. She is wary of men who try to come in and take over.

To me, Sophie is a Type 8.

III

SOPHIE
Frank better figure how to work
for a living! I picked up the new deeds
today. One for you, one for me
and one for Baby Sister. That ought to
make her feel grown.

FANNIE
She's not going to believe it.

SOPHIE
Why? I always told her she'd have her
share officially when she got old enough.

FANNIE
Knowing you, I think she thought you
meant about sixty-five! Sometimes I try
to imagine what Baby Sister's life is
like over there. How it feels.
It must be exciting. Museums and theatres
all over the place. She said Frank did a
public recital from his book
and there were fifty people there.

SOPHIE
How many colored people were there?

FANNIE
She didn't say.

SOPHIE

None! No! Two! Her and Frank. Who ever heard of a colored poet moving someplace where there aren't any colored people?

FANNIE

Where do you expect him to live? Nicodemus?

SOPHIE

Why not? I'm not giving her the deed to one-third of the land we're standing on and she's married to a man who'd rather take a tour of Piccadilly Circus!

FANNIE

Some people are not raised for this kind of life.

SOPHIE

Did we raise Min for the life she's living halfway around the world?

FANNIE

Of course we did. We always exposed her to the finest things.

SOPHIE

But why do all those fine things have to be so far away from Negroes?

FANNIE

I think our baby sister is having so much
fun out there in the world, coming back
here is probably the last thing on her
mind.

SOPHIE

Do you know how much land they could be
buying with all that money they're
running through living so high on the
hog?

FANNIE

They've got plenty of time to buy land

SOPHIE

All that money and the best he can think
of to do with it is move to England and
print up some books of bad poetry.

Chapter 9
The Peacemaker

(GIGGLING)

Type 9 is the Peacemaker. This personality type likes to keep the peace, goes with the flow to avoid conflict, has trouble saying no, and sometimes feels like their voice has not been heard. Type 9s are also called the mediator, the harmonizer, or the connector. They like things to be settled and to feel things are settled in themselves. Type 9s are the glue that holds families, communities, and organizations together. They are usually quite skilled in that regard, especially if they're relatively self-aware.

The key goal for Type 9s is harmony—the foundation stone for the energy of this personality type. They like to feel harmonious within themselves and want to feel harmony in whatever group they interact with. They dislike conflict and don't like upsetting other people; they would rather walk away from an argument if there is one looming. There are some instances when a person may need to stand their ground; Type 9s can find this very challenging. When faced with having to deal with something difficult, they will protect themselves by removing themselves from the conversation or situation.

Type 9s are good at building consensus and mediating when they put their mind and energy into it. They like to accept other people and their views even if they are different from their own, and out of all of the personality types, Type 9s seem to be incredibly wise in many ways because they can easily understand the different views of the other people. They are amazing in how they do it—it's both a gift and a curse. The challenging part is if they see some value in the perspective of several people about the same thing, it can be enormously difficult for them to make up their mind, which can lead to procrastination and indecision until they've worked it out in their mind.

Finding You in Every Script

Being an instinctual type, they tend to contain their physical energy. They like to feel calm in their physical body, in their minds, and in their emotions. If those elements of themselves get disrupted, it can be pretty disturbing for a Type 9.

One of the special gifts of Type 9s is that they have the ability to bring people together; they are the bridge builders. They build consensus, compromise well, and build compromise. They are caring and attentive to others. People like being around Type 9s because they are great listeners and understand different viewpoints. They can see the eight other personality types and find a commonality with those perspectives in order to bring people together. They are patient, calm, and can bring peace and harmony to sometimes difficult circumstances.

Type 9s provide a pleasant and comfortable atmosphere for people to work in. They are easygoing, consistent, collaborative, and supportive of others. They are good at talking things through and have a habitability to structure and bring attention to detail to the group.

To lessen the chances of being viewed as weak-minded or a pushover, Type 9s should practice standing in their power and being more assertive when required. If conflict presents itself, step into it instead of shying away from it. They have a physical reaction to conflict when it arises. It doesn't mean they can't deal with conflict; it's just a very discomforting experience for them.

Although they can focus on priorities, sometimes they can get scattered in their minds about what's important and what's not. Still, if they are clear and concise with their communication, then they can make it easy for people to understand what's expected of them. They are good at delegating and getting things done. However, there can be a sense of wanting to do things themselves so as not to overwhelm or overload their people.

Avoidance of conflict is a challenge for a Type 9 personality. Not dealing with things when they are happening temporarily "saves the day" in terms of not having to experience the discomfort of the person or situation. However, that often means the issue is going to grow crocodile teeth and bite them later. Instead, they need to muscle up, be more vocal, and deal with those things that are causing them and others discomfort.

Their indecisiveness is partly driven by their beautiful perception and understanding of the different perspectives of the other types. They know if they agree with one perspective, they will upset some people, and they don't like upsetting anyone. This can make it tough being a Type 9 sometimes, but they try to remain calm. Their energy is beautiful, but they often hide their discomfort and concerns. Instead, they need to work on finding their voice, speaking up, and letting people know what their views are concerning the issues at hand. Type 9s can become so wrapped up in trying to keep the peace with others that they often neglect things that need attention in their own lives—both business and personal.

All the personality types have derailers, but when Type 9s avoid conflict, they pull back instead of moving forward. They are being indecisive and procrastinating. They are not letting people know their views when they should be voicing them. They are not serving anybody if they sit around doing nothing and not making decisions. If pushed too hard by others, they will dig their heels in and be as stubborn as a mule on the Grand Canyon, not budging.

Another trigger for Type 9s is having a hard time saying no. It is extremely hard for them take a position when they know there will be some opposition. Following through on a commitment they don't really want to do can cause enormous stress.

Type 9s get angry, but you usually won't witness it unless you know them well or it gets to a boiling point. Things that can make a Type 9 angry are unfairness and being pushed too hard into an uncomfortable position. Being forced to do something they don't want to do can anger them. In a professional setting, they might say yes when they want nothing more than to tell the person no. The act of going along just to get along can start to have an impact on their physical bodies and state of mind. Instead of holding it all in, they need to find ways of expressing themselves. They don't need to be overtly angry, but they certainly need to express their point of view.

Type 9s often talk about their feelings of not being heard, which is important to them. You can get the best out of a Type 9 by actively listening and asking questions, particularly about how they're feeling. Once you ask those questions, they will open up, and a lot of stuff will come pouring out. There may be a lot of passive aggression, but you can help them to work that out. Take the time to create a pleasant environment, as they like to be comfortable. Help them take action, and show them by your actions that you value their contribution.

Type 9s are not out there tooting their own horn. They are quiet achievers. Make sure they are recognized for their contribution. Type 9s can exhibit some Type 6 traits when stressed; some of those debilitating characteristics will be doubt and confusion. Self-doubt will come up as well as cynicism or skepticism.

When a Type 9 is happy and relaxed, they go to Nike Zone, Type 3. Just DO it! They know what they need to do. They've done the analysis and have worked it out in their head. Now all they have to do is put things in motion and get it done. Once they get into a "Just do it" mindset, they're even more productive than the Type 3s because there is none of that "Look at me" or "I want the recognition or the reward." They are focused on getting the job done because they see it as them being responsible and committed. This mood is a great place for a Type 9 to be.

I have found Type 9 leaders to be great. One, in particular, is our friend and pastor, who is very caring, humble, and diplomatic in nature. He is such a likeable person, funny and easy-going. He likes to make everyone feel comfortable, like they are family. Everyone feels seen and heard when in his presence. He takes everyone's ideas and opinions into account when making decisions. He is calm and patient when making what he believes is the right decision for all. He could easily run for a political office and win. He is a leader for the people, a public servant, and has "the feet of peace."

By developing their self-awareness, Type 9s will find themselves in a calmer place and better able to manage life's challenges. When they self-observe, they give themselves opportunities to find their voices and are more able to speak on their desires, needs, and opinions. Type 9s need to acknowledge their own needs and express them. They should pay attention to their feelings and actively deal with the ramifications of those feelings instead of allowing them to fester, ultimately causing bigger problems. They will do themselves a great deal of good if they determine their priorities and follow through on them, even if there is some discomfort or conflict in the process.

Because of all the stress they may experience due to always trying to play peacemaker, Type 9s should prioritize looking after their physical bodies. They need to exercise and eat moderately. When they're under stress, Type 9s tend to indulge in not-so-healthy comfort food. Sometimes their diet will consist of foods high in sugar and fat, which we know can be harmful to the human body and result in a person becoming sick with certain illnesses and physical ailments.

That being said, for the sake of your well-being, it would behoove Type 9s to find your voice and step into your power.

Character Example of Type 8: The Peacemaker

An Overview of

INTIMATE APPAREL by Pearle Cleage

Set in 1905 in turn of the century New York, *Intimate Apparel* tells the story of Esther, a lonely, single African-American woman who makes her living sewing beautiful corsets and ladies' undergarments. There is warm affection between her and the Orthodox Jewish man who sells fabrics to her, but any relationship between them, even a touch, is completely forbidden. Seeking love and romance, Esther eventually embarks on a letter-writing relationship with a mysterious suitor on the Panama Canal to which she accepts his proposal for marriage. After his arrival to New York, the marriage soon turns sour and leads Esther to realize that only her self-reliance and certainty of her own worth will see her through life's challenges.

Esther exhibits traits of a Type 9.

MARKS

I have something else to show you. It's
here. Where is it? Where are you? Here we
are.

(Unfurls a roll of Valenciennes lace)

I almost let it go last week, but I was
waiting for you. I wanted you to see it.

ESTHER

(smiling) Oh, yes.

MARKS

I knew you'd like it. *(Elated)* The wait
was worth seeing your smile again.

*(Mr. Marks playfully drapes the lace
around Esther's neck. They find themselves
standing dangerously close to each other.
They are so close they can inhale each
other's words.)*

Miss Mills, if I may say——

ESTHER

Armstrong.

(Removes the lace from her shoulders)

MARKS
I apologize. I forget. I forget.

(Mark takes the lace and places it on the cutting board.)

ESTHER
It is pretty, thank you. But today I've come for fabric for a gentleman's suit. Next time.

MARKS
Yes. Just a minute. I have some other wools, gabardine, if you'd like to see. I have no story for them, but they are sturdy and reliable, will give you no problems.

(As Marks turns to search for another bolt of fabric, Esther gently runs her fingers across the lace. Marks turns with the dark, drab suit fabrics. He slowly rolls the lace, his disappointment palpable.)

Next time.

ESTHER
Mr. Marks?

MARKS
Yes?

(Esther wants to say something, but she can't quite find the words.)

Is there——?

ESTHER
No. No… I'm sorry… I can't do this.
(Distraught) I thought I'd be able to,
but I can't. I can't come here anymore.
I——

MARKS
Why do you say this? Did I do something
to offend, tell me, did I——

ESTHER
No.

MARKS
Then——

ESTHER
Please, I think you know why.

(A moment.)

MARKS
How many yards will you need for the
gentleman's suit?

Finding You in Every Script

ESTHER

Four yards. The Scottish wool…and if you
would, please wrap the Valenciennes lace.

The Finale

The finale or big takeaway from all this talk about personality types is getting people to understand the importance of self-awareness and empathy for others. Self-awareness is a critical competency regardless of the role a person aspires to be in life. Paying attention to your thoughts, feelings, and behavioral impulses can be used to your advantage to achieve your objectives in life. Empathy is essential for building healthy relationships. It doesn't just happen; healthy relationships are intentional when you choose to understand others. Knowing your personality type can take you to a level of self-awareness, self-acceptance, and self-love that you only dreamed of reaching, and you will also be able to extend the same to others. When you seek awareness and empathy, you can truly "love your neighbor the same as you love yourself." (Mark 12:31)

Using self-awareness and empathy to become a better actor can be a matter of just rehearsing who you want to become—the "you" in your story or script. Rehearse in your mind how "you" would walk, talk, eat, breathe, and smile as a Type 1 or 7. How would "you" would greet people or conduct yourself during a Zoom call as a Type 9 or 5? How would "you" handle being stuck in rush-hour traffic on a Friday when all you want is to get to the comfort of your home after having a nerve-racking week at the job as a Type 4 or 2?

When you close your eyes and mentally rehearse the role or type, and if you're truly present, the brain will not know the difference between the real-life "you" and the "you" that you imagine yourself to be. The rehearsal process can trick the brain into thinking you've already experienced it and you are who you imagine yourself to be. The hardware is in place; now, all you have to do is step into the footprints. Keep doing it until it becomes a software program. Keep acting "as if," and everything will begin to change. Your energy will change, the way you walk will change, the way you breathe will change, and so on. You will become someone new, someone different. When you condition the body and the mind to believe you *are* that person, that's when you become that person. There is no difference between "you" and "you" in the script. You become authentically you in every story and therefore can

Finding You in Every Script

handle every script because there is nothing in the script but "you".

Look for yourself in the script. Find you in the script. Release you. Mold you. Unlock you. You hold the key. You have the secret. The secret is "You."

Stay Connected with Shaunté Online

Official Website

www.shauntemassard.com

Instagram

www.instagram.com/i_am_shaunte

Facebook

www.facebook.com/shauntemassard

Twitter

www.twitter.com/shauntemassard

LinkedIn

www.linkedin.com/in/shauntemassard

CPSIA information can be obtained
at www.ICGtesting.com
Printed in the USA
BVHW011127140223
658482BV00021B/523